U.S. HISTORY IN REVIEW

Women's Suffrage

BY KATHRYN WALTON

Please visit our website, www.enslow.com. For a free color catalog of all our high-quality books, call toll free 1-800-398-2504 or fax 1-877-980-4454.

Library of Congress Cataloging-in-Publication Data
Names: Walton, Kathryn, 1993- author.
Title: Women's suffrage / Kathryn Walton.
Description: Buffalo, New York : Enslow Publishing, [2024] | Series: U.S.
  history in review | Includes bibliographical references and index.
Identifiers: LCCN 2023010111 (print) | LCCN 2023010112 (ebook) | ISBN
  9781978536241 (library binding) | ISBN 9781978536234 (paperback) | ISBN
  9781978536258 (ebook)
Subjects: LCSH: Women–Suffrage–United States–Juvenile literature. |
  Voting–United States–Juvenile literature. | United
  States–History–Juvenile literature.
Classification: LCC JK1898 .W3 2024 (print) | LCC JK1898 (ebook) | DDC
  324.6/230973–dc23/eng/20230302
LC record available at https://lccn.loc.gov/2023010111
LC ebook record available at https://lccn.loc.gov/2023010112

Published in 2024 by
Enslow Publishing
2544 Clinton Street
Buffalo, NY 14224

Copyright © 2024 Enslow Publishing

Portions of this work were originally authored by Seth Lynch and published as *Womens Suffrage*. All new material in this edition is authored by Kathryn Walton.

Designer: Leslie Taylor
Editor: Natalie Humphrey

Photo credits: Cover Everett Collection/Shutterstock.com; series art (grunge flag) Andrey Kuzmin/Shutterstock.com; series art (stamp icon) Stocker_team/Shutterstock.com; series art (font) santstock/Shutterstock.com; p. 5 Everett Collection/Shutterstock.com; p. 6 Ink Drop/Shutterstock.com; p. 7 Everett Collection/Shutterstock.com; p. 9 Alizada Studios/Shutterstock.com; p. 10 Everett Collection/Shutterstock.com; p. 11 Lucretia Mott and Elizabeth Cady Stanton/https://commons.wikimedia.org/wiki/File:Women%27s_Rights_Convention_attendees.jpg; p. 13 Everett Collection/Shutterstock.com; p. 15 Everett Collection/Shutterstock.com; p. 16 U.S. Capitol/https://commons.wikimedia.org/wiki/File:Flickr_-_USCapitol_-_Lincoln%27s_Second_Inaugural,_1865.jpg; p. 17 Everett Collection/Shutterstock.com; p. 19 Everett Collection/Shutterstock.com; p. 20 Unknown Author/https://commons.wikimedia.org/wiki/File:Women_practice_voting_in_Dayton_Oct._27,_1920.jpg; p. 21 (top) Yavuz ILDIZ/Shutterstock.com, (bottom) MM_photos/Shutterstock.com; p. 23 Everett Collection/Shutterstock.com; p. 25 Author Unknown/LOC.com; p. 26 MM_photos/Shutterstock.com; p. 27 Everett Collection/Shutterstock.com; p. 29 Png Studio Photography/Shutterstock.com.

All rights reserved. No part of this book may be reproduced in any form without permission in writing from the publisher, except by a reviewer.

Printed in the United States of America

CPSIA compliance information: Batch #CSENS24: For further information, contact Enslow Publishing at 1-800-398-2504.

Find us on

Contents

The Right to Vote 4
The Seneca Falls Convention 8
More Conventions 12
The Civil War 14
The National Woman Suffrage
    Association 18
The Fight Continues 22
A New Era of Suffragists 24
The Future of Women's Rights 28
Timeline 30
Glossary 31
For More Information 32
Index 32

Words in the glossary appear in **bold** the first time they are used in the text.

The Right to Vote

In the early 1800s, not everyone in the United States had suffrage, or the right to vote. Many U.S. women wanted to make changes in the country. But they didn't have the right to vote, and the government wouldn't listen to them.

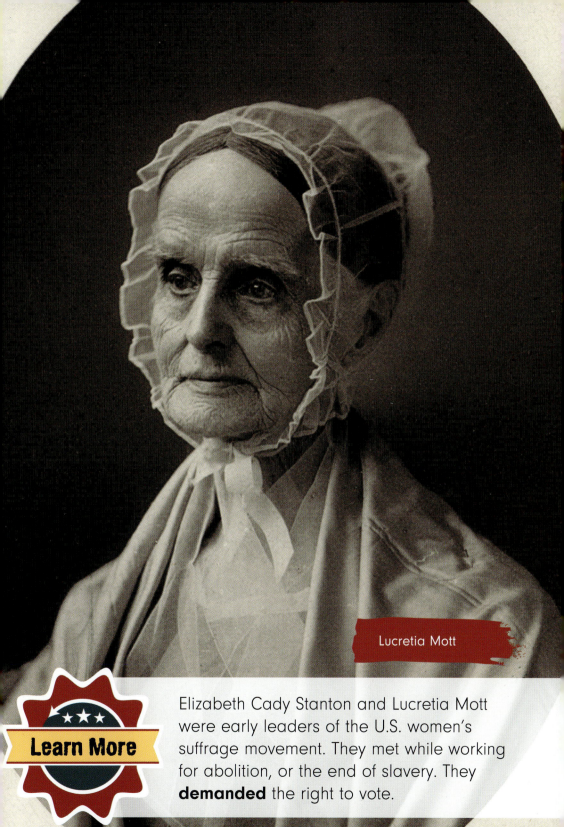

Lucretia Mott

Learn More

Elizabeth Cady Stanton and Lucretia Mott were early leaders of the U.S. women's suffrage movement. They met while working for abolition, or the end of slavery. They **demanded** the right to vote.

People talked about women's rights in the United States for years before the women's suffrage movement. But historians say the true beginning of this movement was 1848. That year, Mott, Stanton, and three other women held a **convention** for women's rights.

Elizabeth Cady Stanton

Learn More

Elizabeth Cady Stanton was born in 1815. She had more schooling than most girls at the time. She also learned about law from her father.

The Seneca Falls Convention

To spread the word for the convention, the women placed an ad in newspapers. News of the convention also traveled by word of mouth. The convention happened on July 19 and 20, 1848. It took place in Seneca Falls, New York.

Around 300 people went to the convention. Most of the people who went were women, but around 40 men went too!

At the convention, Stanton presented the Declaration of Sentiments. This **document** stated the rights women should have. It asked for the right to schooling and equal treatment under the law. It also demanded the right to vote in government.

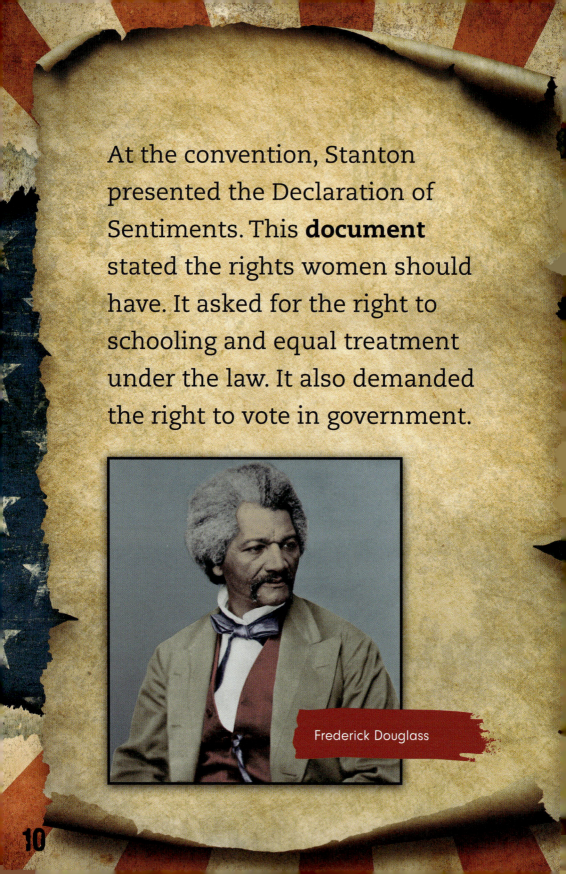

Frederick Douglass

Our Roll of Honor

Containing all the Signatures to the "Declaration of Sentiments" Set Forth by the First

Woman's Rights Convention,

held at

Seneca Falls, New York

July 19-20, 1848

LADIES:

Lucretia Mott
Harriet Cady Eaton
Margaret Pryor
Elizabeth Cady Stanton
Eunice Newton Foote
Mary Ann M'Clintock
Margaret Schooley
Martha C. Wright
Jane C. Hunt
Amy Post
Catherine F. Stebbins
Mary Ann Frink
Lydia Mount
Delia Mathews
Catherine C. Paine
Elizabeth W. M'Clintock
Malvina Seymour
Phebe Mosher
Catherine Shaw
Deborah Scott
Sarah Hallowell
Mary M'Clintock
Mary Gilbert

Sophronia Taylor
Cynthia Davis
Hannah Plant
Lucy Jones
Sarah Whitney
Mary H. Hallowell
Elizabeth Conklin
Sally Pitcher
Mary Conklin
Susan Quinn
Mary S. Mirror
Phebe King
Julia Ann Drake
Charlotte Woodward
Martha Underhill
Dorothy Mathews
Eunice Barker
Sarah R. Woods
Lydia Gild
Sarah Hoffman
Elizabeth Leslie
Martha Ridley

Rachel D. Bonnel
Betsey Tewksbury
Rhoda Palmer
Margaret Jenkins
Cynthia Fuller
Mary Martin
P. A. Culvert
Susan R. Doty
Rebecca Race
Sarah A. Mosher
Mary E. Vail
Lucy Spalding
Lovina Latham
Sarah Smith
Eliza Martin
Maria E. Wilbur
Elizabeth D. Smith
Caroline Barker
Ann Porter
Experience Gibbs
Antoinette E. Segur
Hannah J. Latham
Sarah Sisson

GENTLEMEN:

Richard P. Hunt
Samuel D. Tillman
Justin Williams
William Burroughs
Robert Smallbridge
Jacob Mathews
Charles L. Hoskins
Thomas M'Clintock
Jacob P. Chamberlain

William S. Dell
James Mott
William Burroughs
Robert Smallbridge

Nathan J. Milliken
S. E. Woodworth
Edward F. Underhill
George W. Pryor
Joel Bunker
Isaac VanTassel
Thomas Dell
Stephen Shear

Azaliah Schooley

More Conventions

After the Seneca Falls Convention, people held other conventions on women's rights. The first national women's rights convention took place in Massachusetts in 1850. In 1852, Stanton planned another convention with Susan B. Anthony. It was clear that the call for women's suffrage was strong.

Susan B. Anthony

Learn More

Susan B. Anthony was born in Massachusetts on February 15, 1820. She was an abolitionist before she joined the fight for women's right to vote.

The Civil War

In 1861, the fight for women's suffrage stopped for a time. This is because the **Civil War** started. Many women, including Stanton and Anthony, worked in favor of the Thirteenth **Amendment**. This amendment would end slavery. It was **ratified** in December 1865 after the war ended.

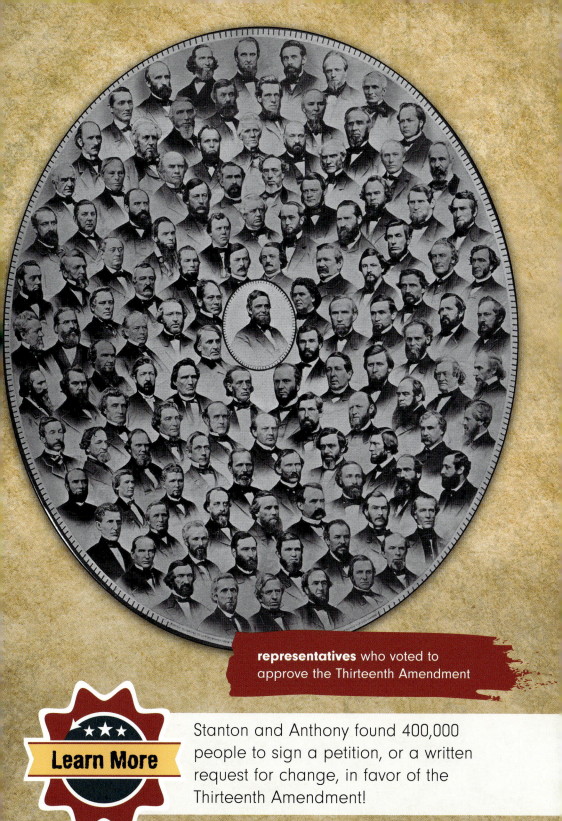

representatives who voted to approve the Thirteenth Amendment

Learn More

Stanton and Anthony found 400,000 people to sign a petition, or a written request for change, in favor of the Thirteenth Amendment!

15

Two more amendments were passed soon after the Civil War. The Fourteenth Amendment gave all adult men **citizenship**, including the right to vote. The Fifteenth Amendment says governments can't stop men from voting because of their race or color. But these amendments didn't include women.

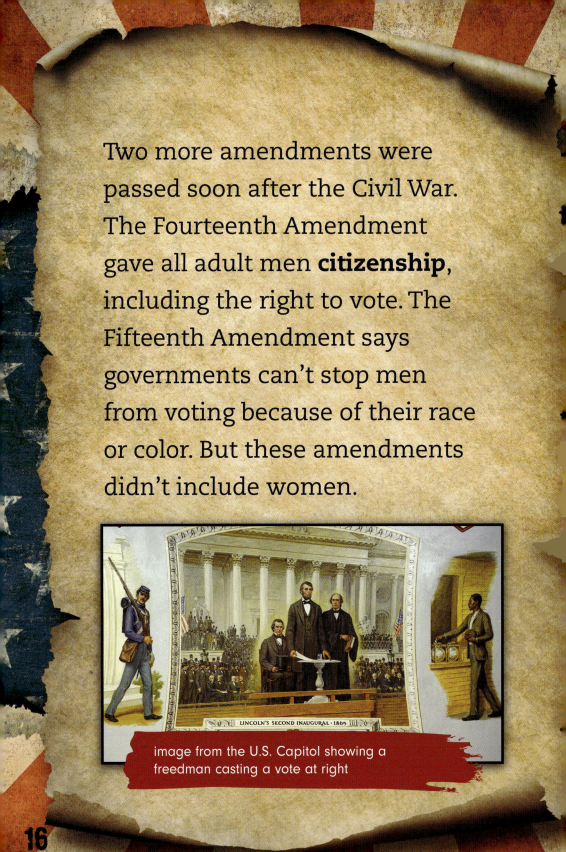

image from the U.S. Capitol showing a freedman casting a vote at right

The Fourteenth Amendment only gave the right to vote to men. It was the first part of the U.S. Constitution to use the word "male."

The National Woman Suffrage Association

Stanton and Anthony started the National Woman Suffrage Association. They worked for a national law giving women suffrage. The American Woman Suffrage Association, formed by Lucy Stone and others, worked toward state laws giving women suffrage.

Learn More

The two groups joined in 1890. They became the National American Woman Suffrage Association (NAWSA).

National American Woman Suffrage Association parade, 1913.

Anthony and about 15 other women voted for president in New York State in November 1872. They were arrested, or taken by the police, but only Anthony went to **trial**. The judge said the wording of the Fourteenth Amendment made it against the law for women to vote.

The judge fined Anthony $100 for voting. Anthony said she would "never pay a dollar" of the fine!

The Fight Continues

In the late 1800s, people presented the first women's suffrage amendments in Congress. They didn't pass. The National Woman Suffrage Association tried to bring an amendment back several times after that. In time, it started to gain favor in Congress.

Learn More

Many states began giving women the right to vote in the late 1800s and early 1900s. That meant Congress was partly **elected** by women. More members of Congress began voting in favor of women's suffrage.

A New Era of Suffragists

In 1900, Carrie Chapman Catt became the president of the NAWSA after Susan B. Anthony. Another suffragist, Alice Paul, left the NAWSA because she wanted to take more action in the fight for women's voting rights. Paul formed the National Women's Party.

The National Women's Party held marches and even hunger strikes in their fight for voting rights. A hunger strike is the act of refusing to eat as a way of showing disagreement with something.

Carrie Chapman Catt

In May 1919, the Nineteenth Amendment passed in the House of Representatives. This amendment would give women the right to vote. It then passed in the Senate in June. The amendment still needed to be ratified by the states before it could become part of the U.S. **Constitution.**

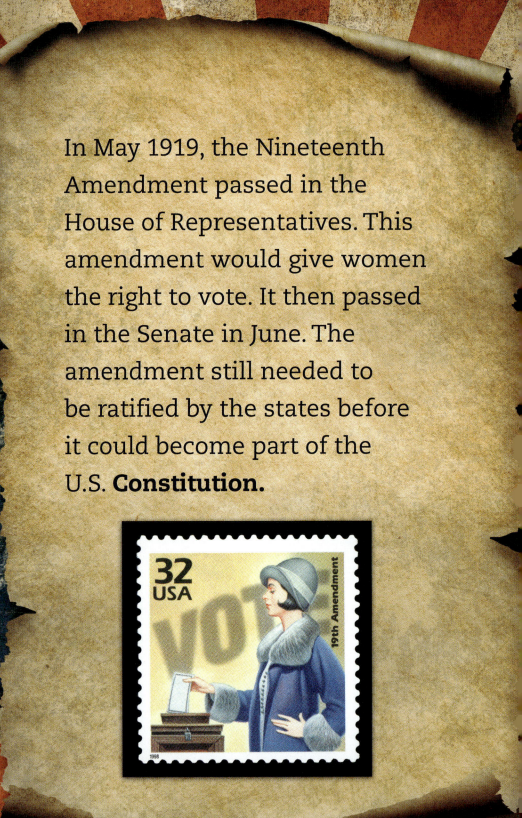

Learn More

The Nineteenth Amendment was ratified by three-fourths of the states in August 1920. After fighting for more than 70 years, the suffragists had won!

The Future of Women's Rights

Even though women now had the right to vote, the suffragists didn't stop fighting! NAWSA became the League of Women Voters. The League of Women Voters works to make sure women have equal rights. It also works to **protect** voting rights for everyone.

Learn More

The National Women's Party **proposed** the Equal Rights Amendment in 1923. This amendment bans **discrimination** based on sex. It still hasn't been ratified in every state.

Timeline

1848
The first convention of the U.S. women's rights movement, the Seneca Falls Convention, is held.

1850
The first national women's rights convention is held in Massachusetts.

1861-1865
The U.S. Civil War takes place.

1868
The Fourteenth Amendment is ratified, and all men are given the right to vote.

1870
The Fifteenth Amendment is ratified, making it illegal to keep someone from voting because of race.

1872
Susan B. Anthony votes in New York State and is arrested.

1918-1919
The Nineteenth Amendment passes in both houses of Congress.

1920
The Nineteenth Amendment is ratified, and women have the right to vote.

Glossary

amendment: A change or addition to a constitution.

citizenship: The state of being a citizen, or someone who lives in a country legally and has certain rights.

Civil War: A war fought from 1861 to 1865 in the United States between the Union (the Northern states) and the Confederacy (the Southern states).

constitution: The basic laws by which a country or state is governed.

convention: A gathering of people who have a common interest or purpose.

demand: To ask forcefully.

discrimination: Unfairly treating people unequally because of their race or beliefs.

document: A formal piece of writing.

elect: To choose for a position in a government.

propose: To offer, or suggest something.

protect: To keep safe.

ratify: To give formal approval for something.

representative: A member of a lawmaking body who acts for voters.

trial: A meeting in a court in which a judge or jury makes decisions according to the law.

For More Information

Books

Harts, Shannon. *Susan B. Anthony and Elizabeth Cady Stanton*. Buffalo, NY: Gareth Stevens Publishing, 2022.

Loh-Hagan, Virginia. *Women's Rights*. Ann Arbor, Michigan: Cherry Lake Publishing, 2022.

Website

National Geographic Kids
kids.nationalgeographic.com/history/article/womens-suffrage-movement
Learn more about the women's rights movement.

Publisher's note to educators and parents: Our editors have carefully reviewed this website to ensure that it is suitable for students. Many websites change frequently, however, and we cannot guarantee that a site's future contents will continue to meet our high standards of quality and educational value. Be advised that students should be closely supervised whenever they access the internet.

Index

abolition, 5, 11, 13
Anthony, Susan B., 13, 14, 15, 18, 20, 21, 24, 30
Catt, Carrie Chapman, 24, 25
Declaration of Sentiments, 10, 11
Equal Rights Amendment, 29
Fifteenth Amendment, 16, 30
Fourteenth Amendment, 16, 17, 20, 30
League of Women Voters, 28
Mott, Lucretia, 5, 6
National American Woman Suffrage Association, 19, 24, 28
National Women's Party, 24, 29
Nineteenth Amendment, 26, 27, 30
Seneca Falls Convention, 6, 7, 8, 9, 12, 30
Stanton, Elizabeth Cady, 5, 6, 7, 12, 14, 15, 18